BAECHLER – MORRISON

BAECHLER
MORRISON

GALLERY ALAIN NOIRHOMME

RUE DE LA RÉGENCE 17 REGENTSCHAPSSTRAAT

BRUSSELS

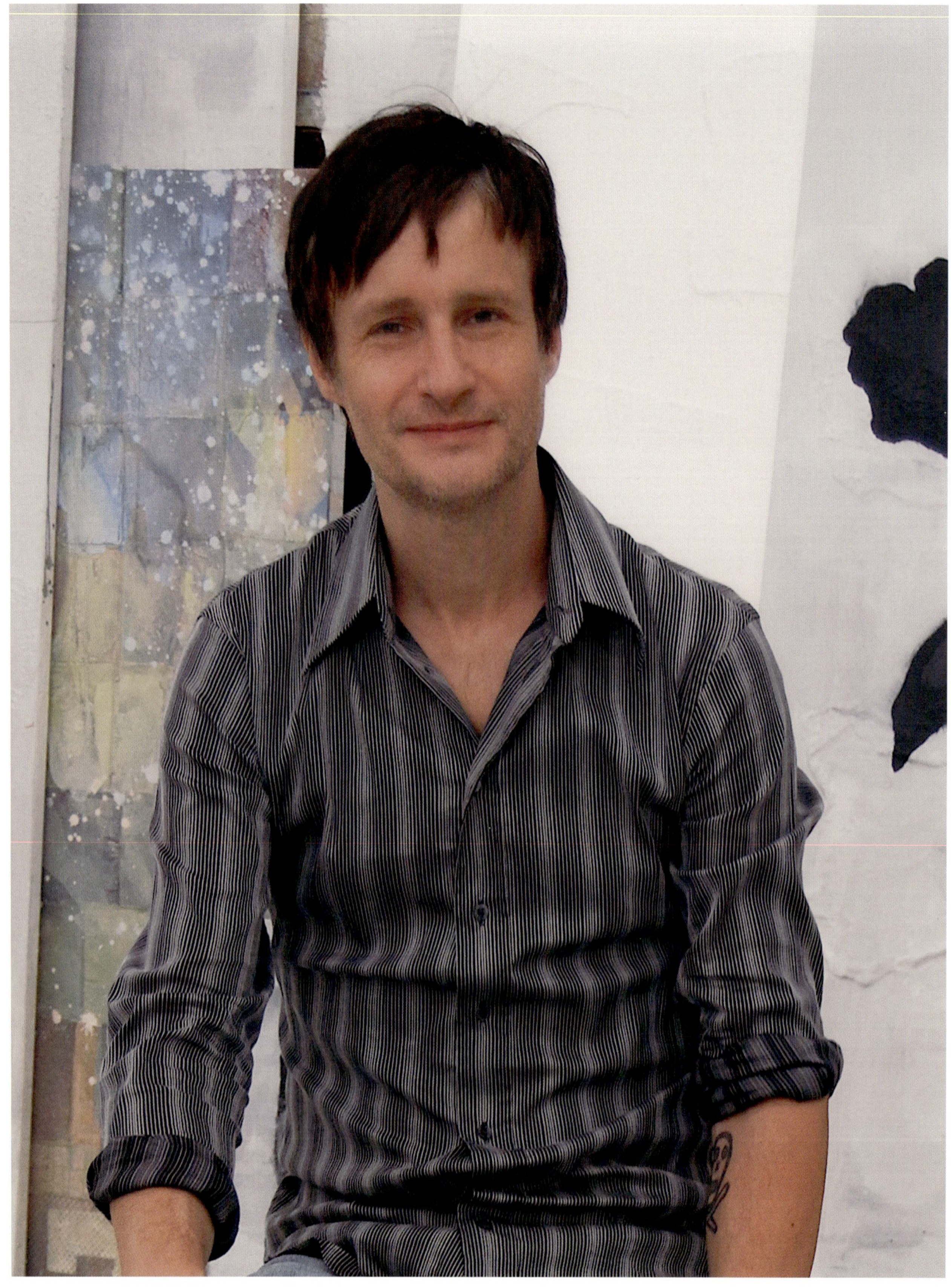

Donald Baechler — Photography by Kevin Baker

DONALD BAECHLER

Donald Baechler

One Kind of Loyalty, 2003

acrylic and fabric collage on canvas

244 x 127 cm

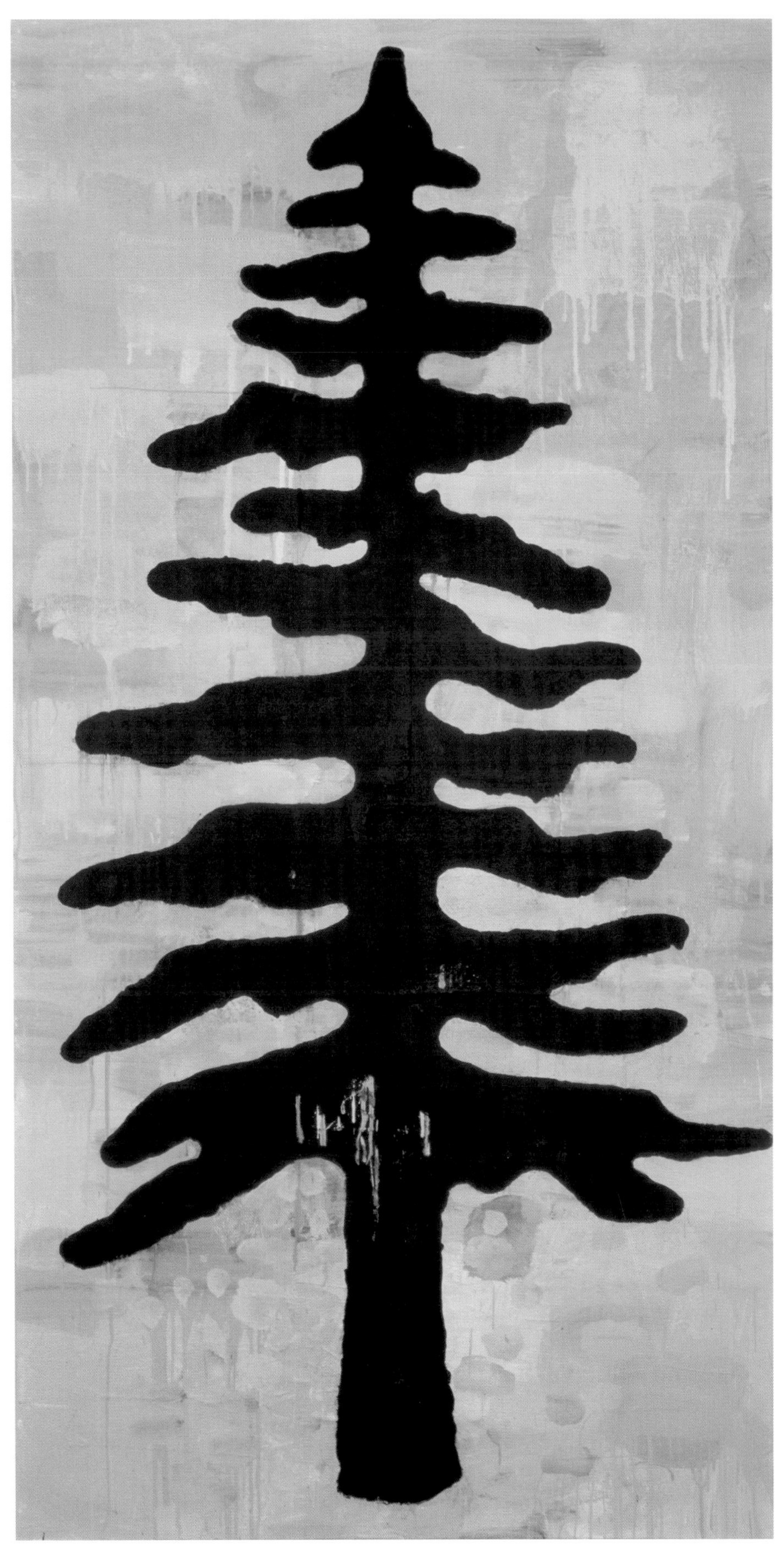

Donald Baechler

A Test of Nerve, 2003

acrylic and fabric collage on canvas

244 x 127 cm

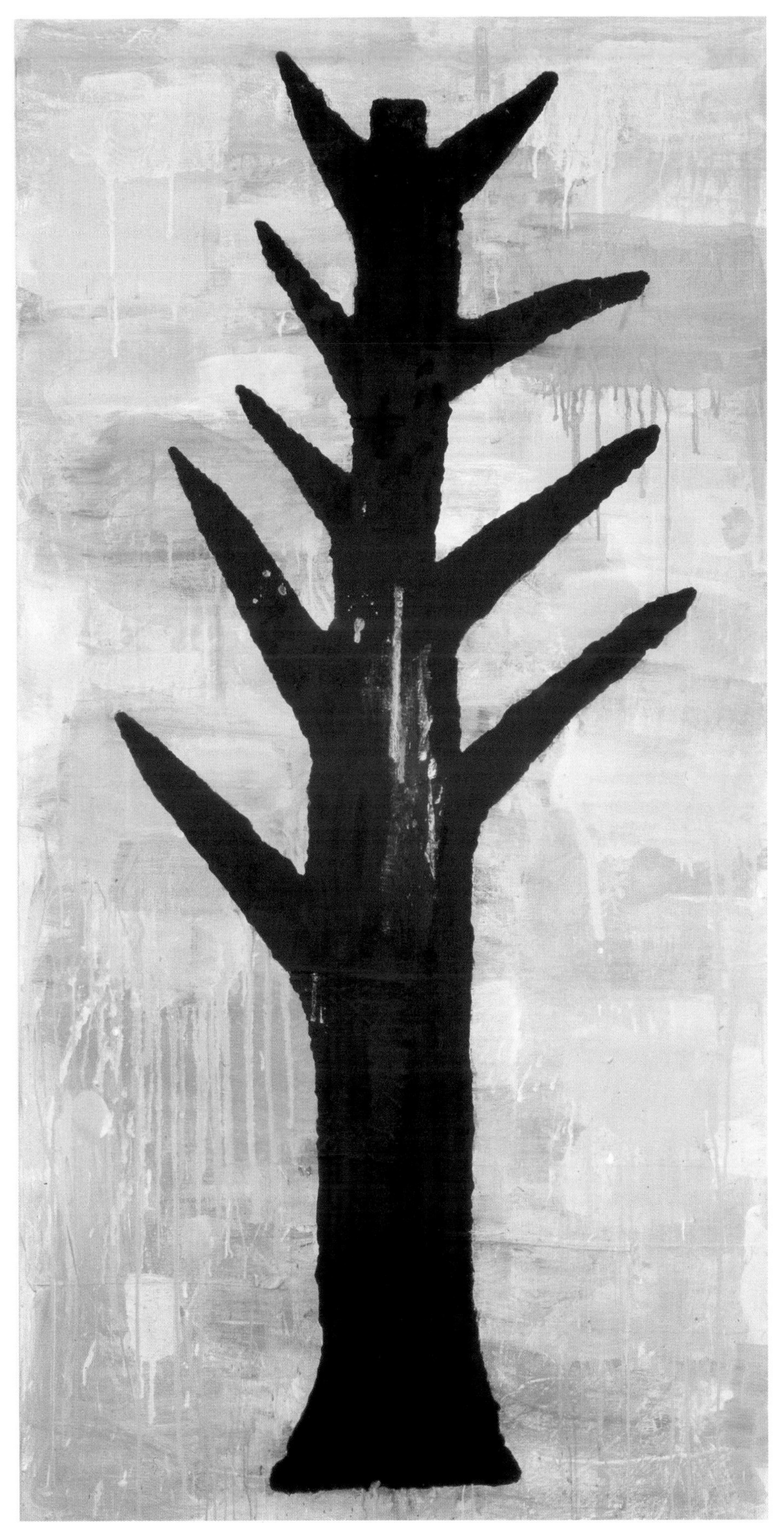

Donald Baechler

Things Happen, 2003

acrylic and fabric collage on canvas

152,5 x 152,5 cm

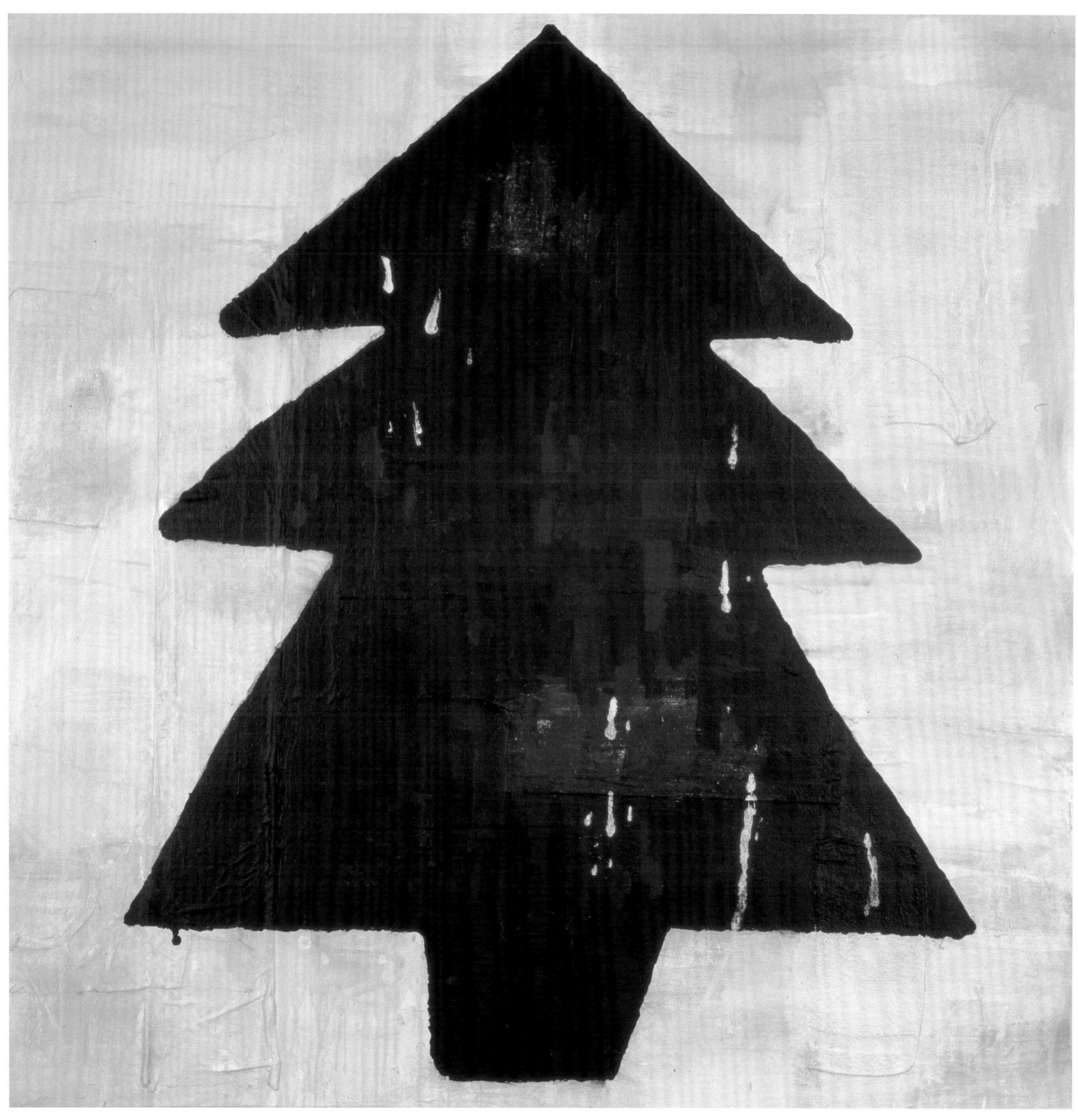

Donald Baechler

The Disappearance #1, 2003

acrylic and fabric collage on canvas

152,5 x 152,5 cm

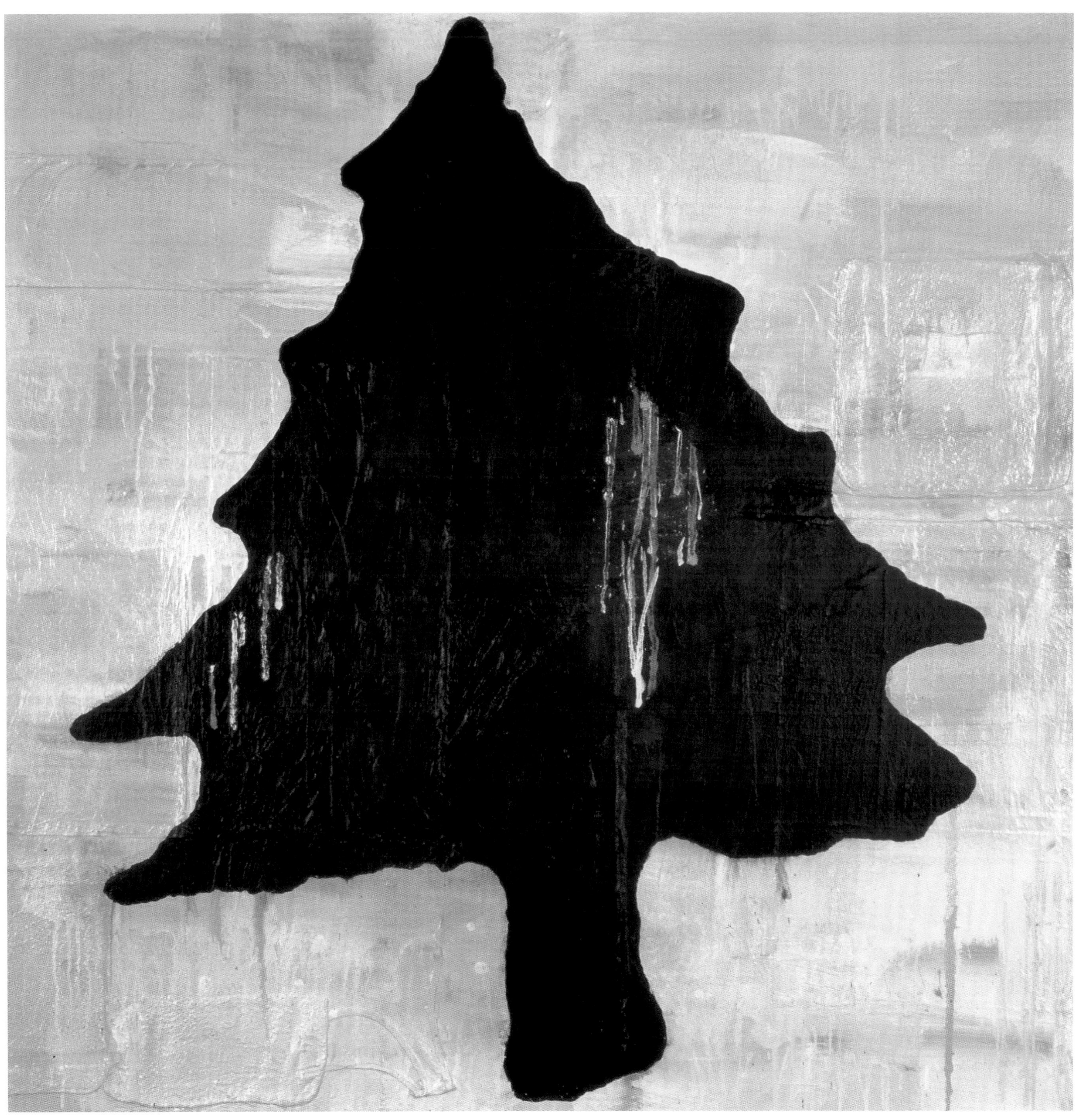

Donald Baechler

Black Tulip, 2003

acrylic and fabric collage on canvas

76 x 61 cm

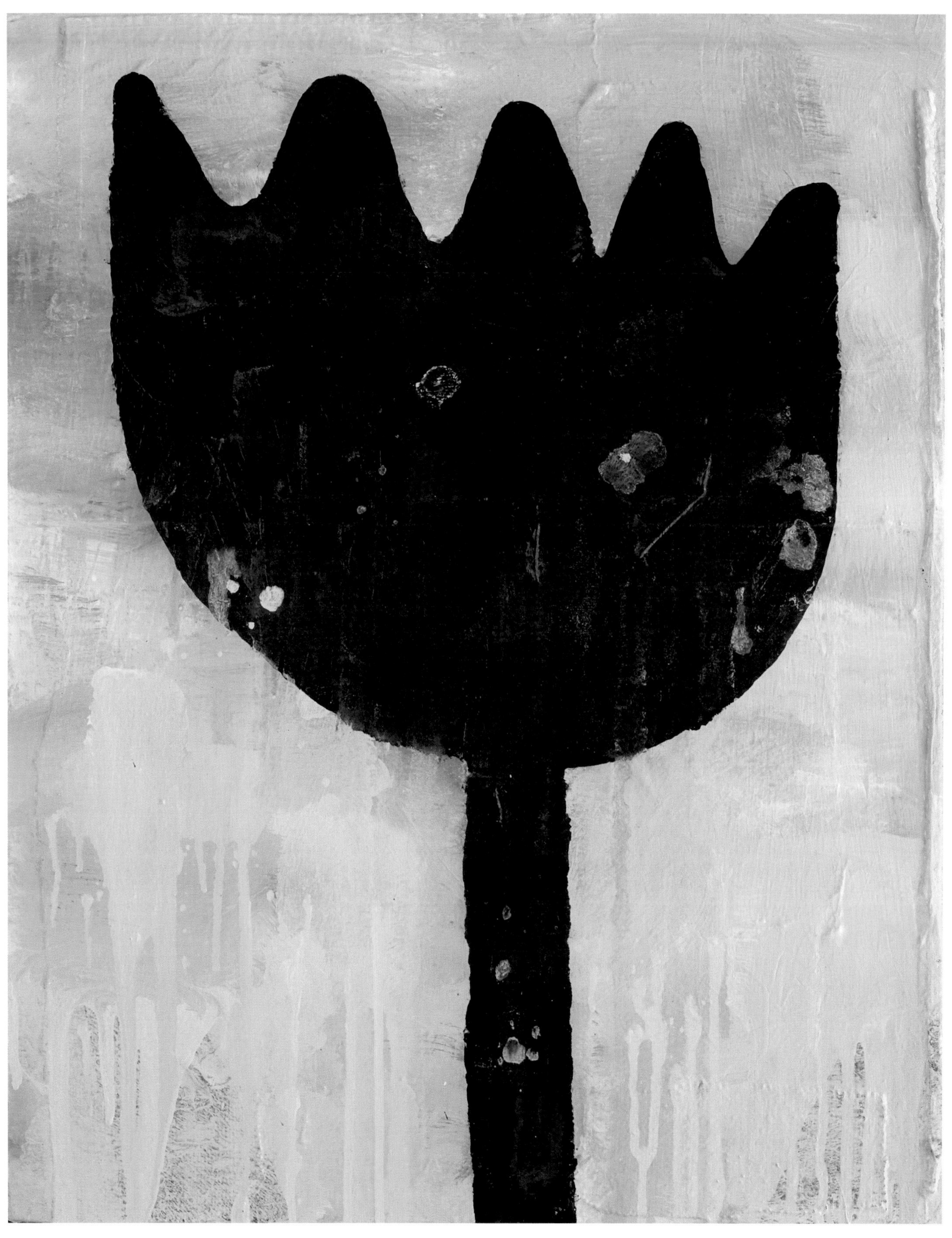

Donald Baechler

Black Tulip, 2003

acrylic and fabric collage on canvas

76 x 61 cm

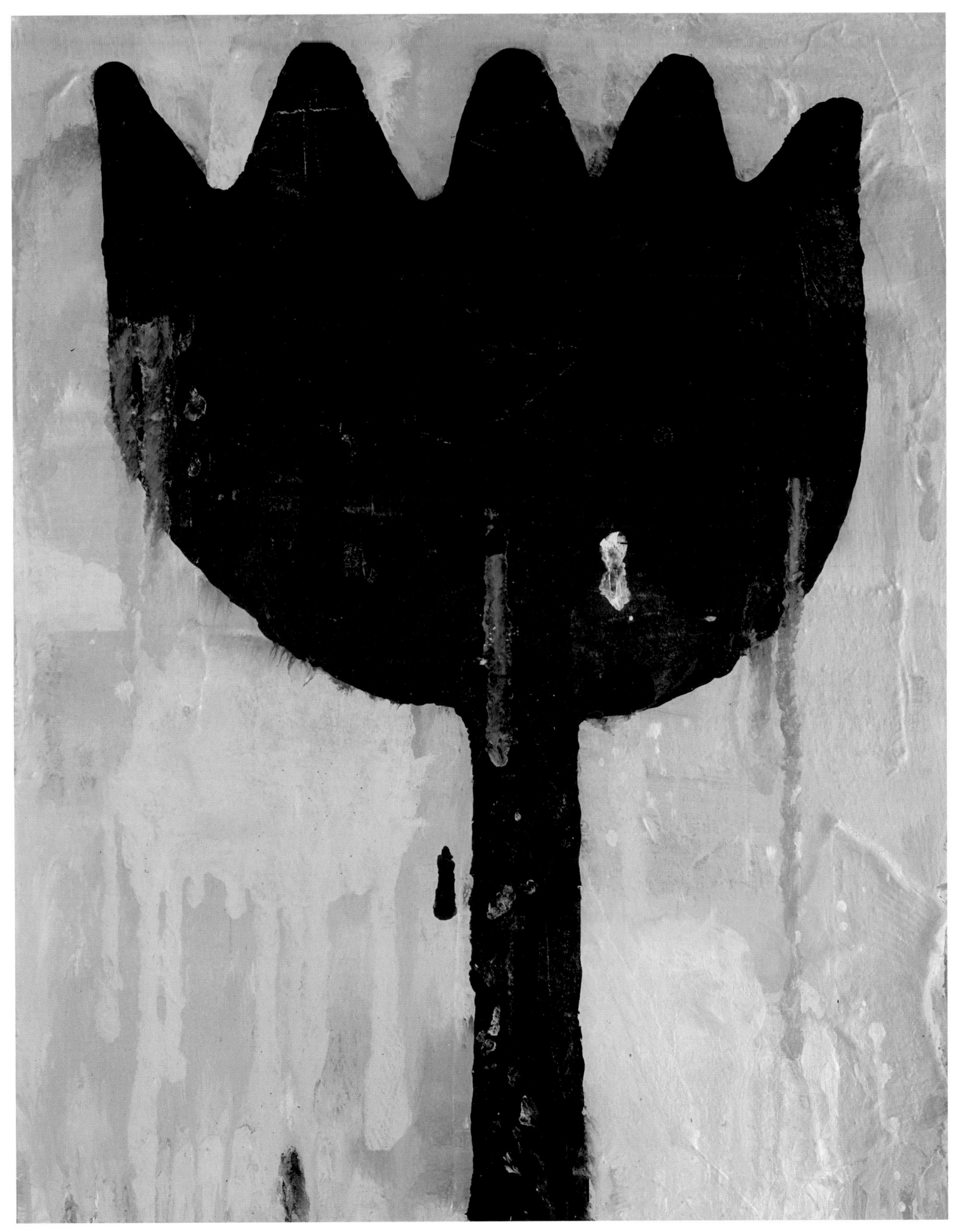

Donald Baechler

Flower Study, 2005

acrylic and fabric collage on canvas

114 x 76 cm

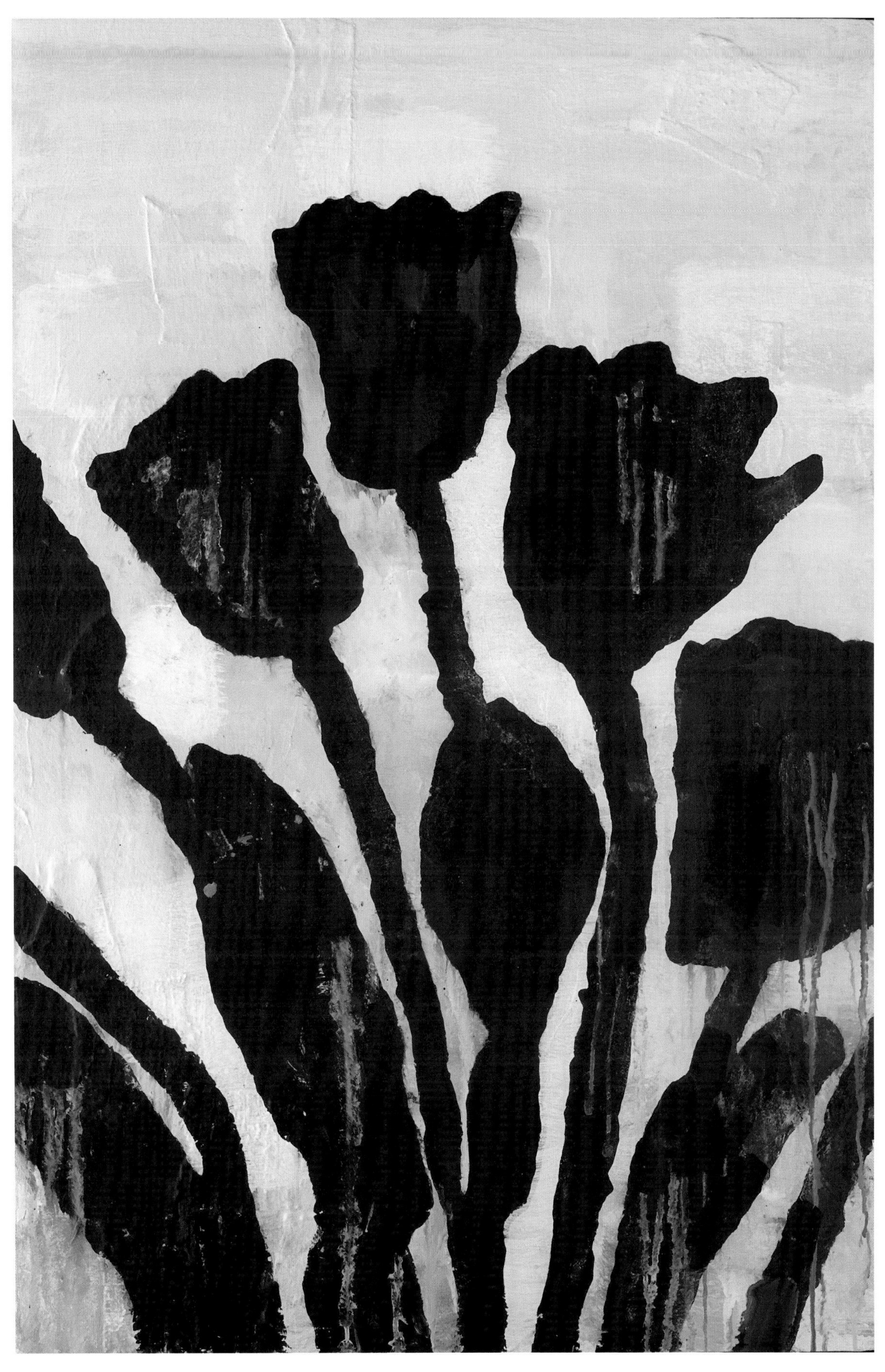

Donald Baechler

Untitled (Flowers), 2007

acrylic and fabric collage on canvas

203 x 163 cm

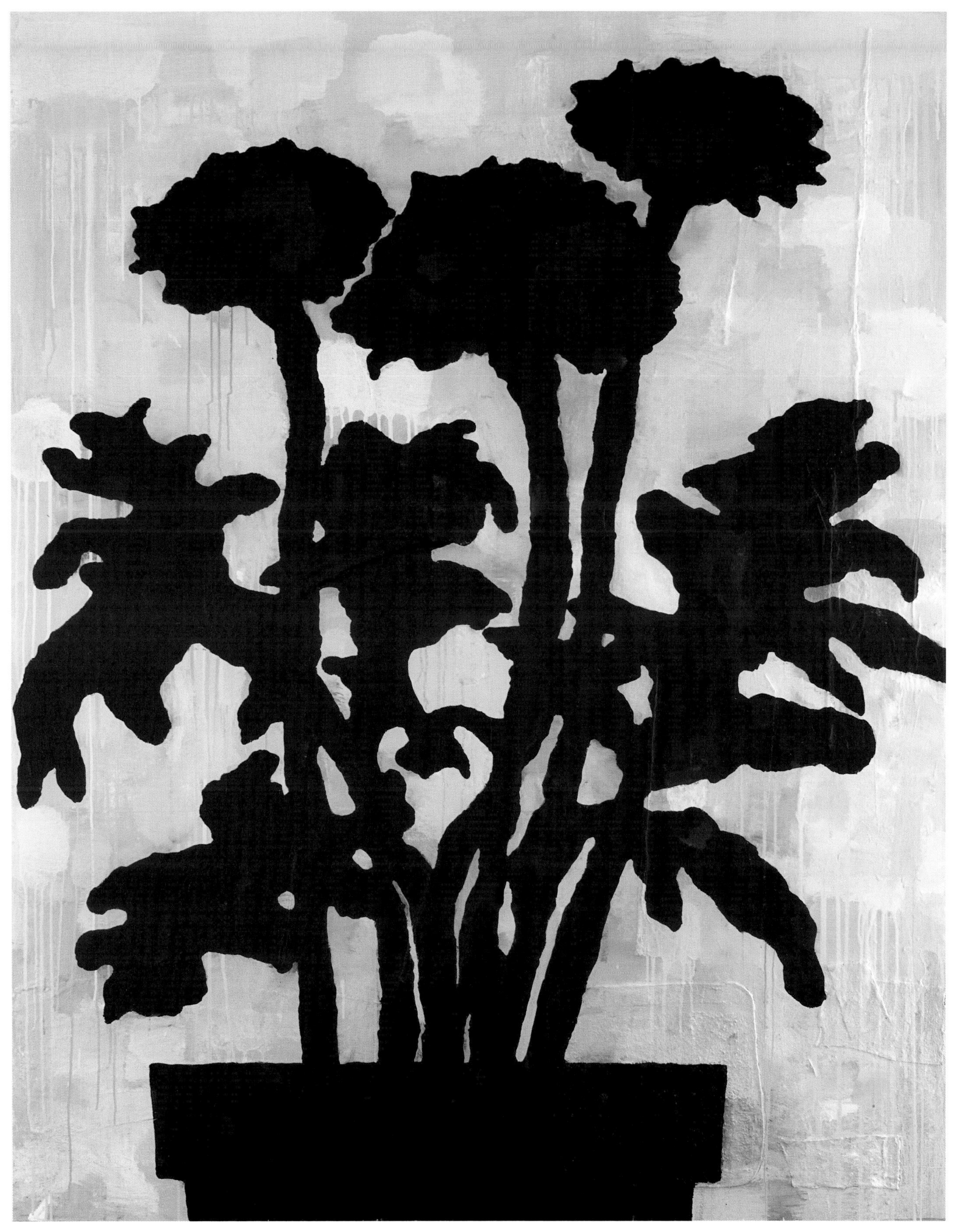

Donald Baechler

Tulips, 2007

acrylic and fabric collage on canvas

114 x 76 cm

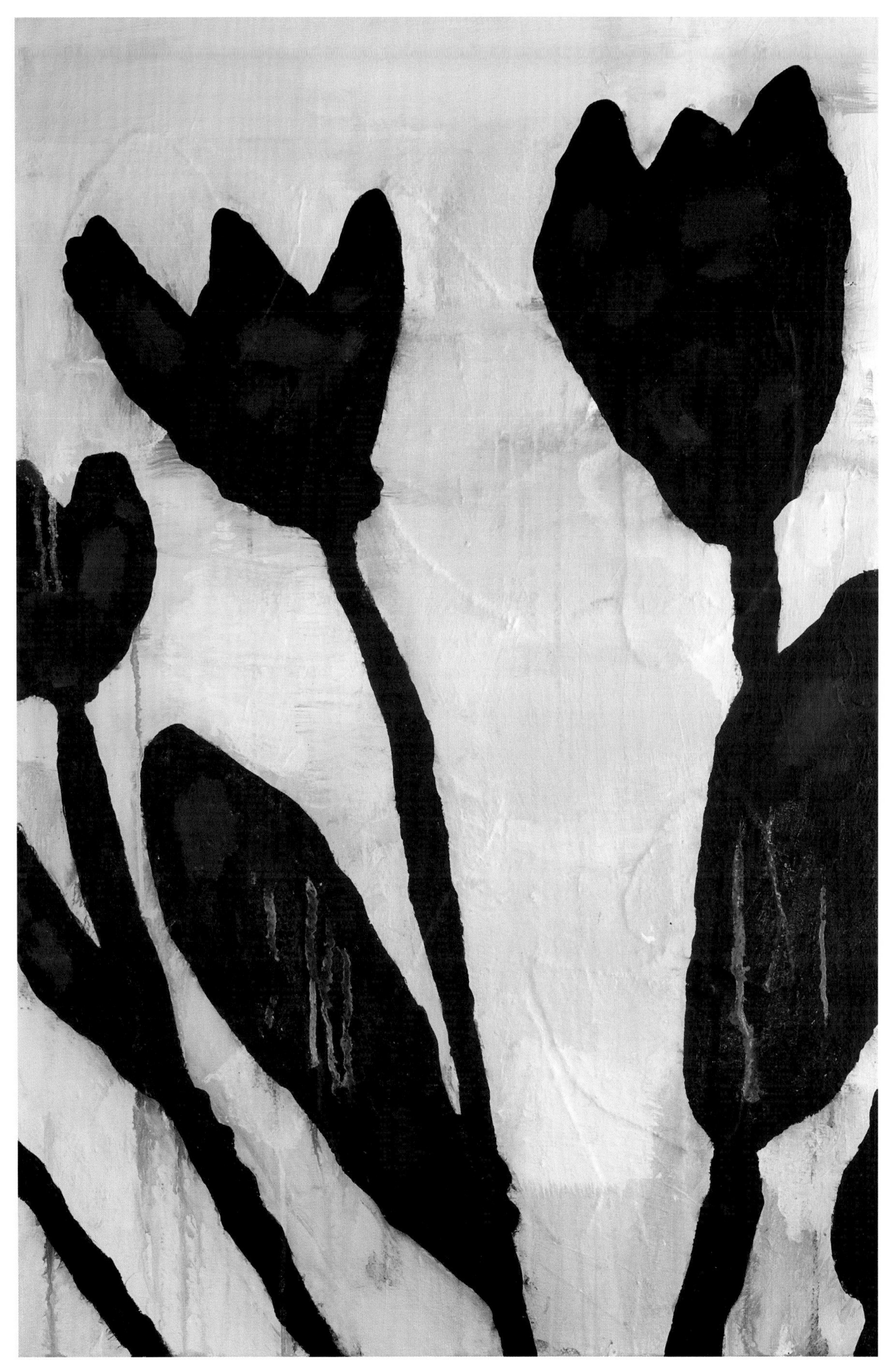

Donald Baechler

Black Flowers, 2007

acrylic and fabric collage on canvas

183 x 122 cm

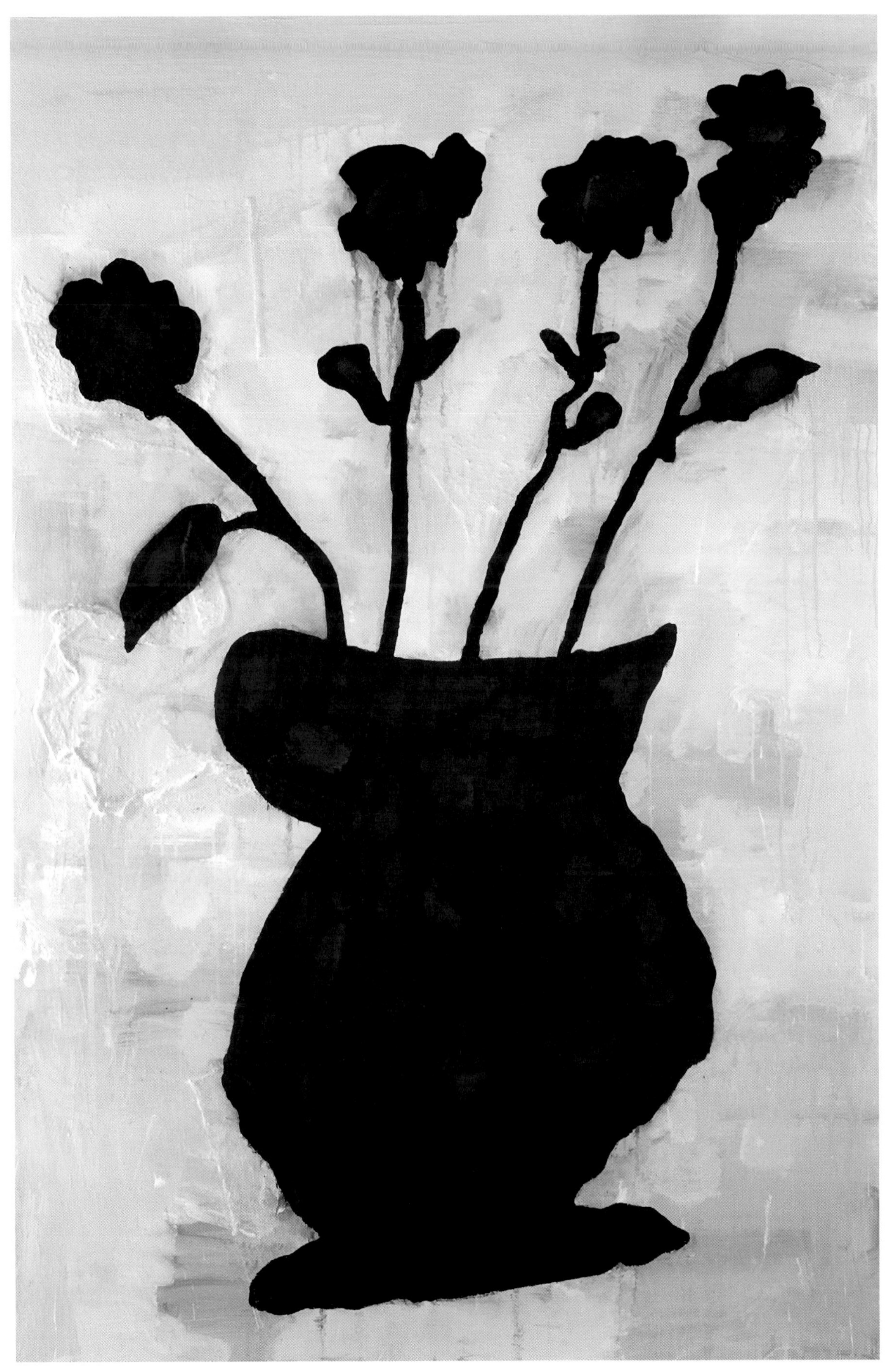

Donald Baechler

Flowers (Cut Sides), 2007

cast bronze

183 x 137 x 7 cm

Ed. of 8

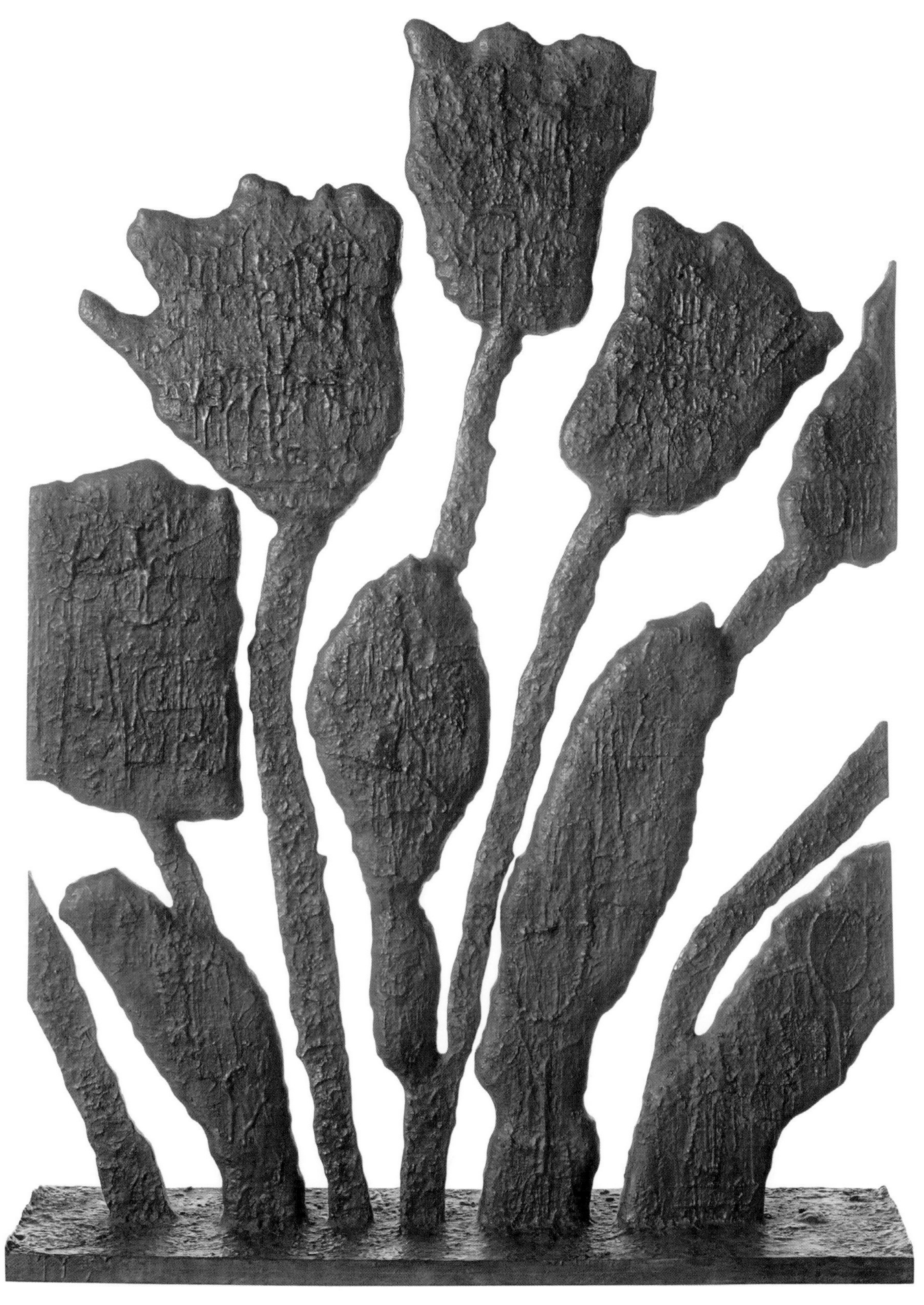

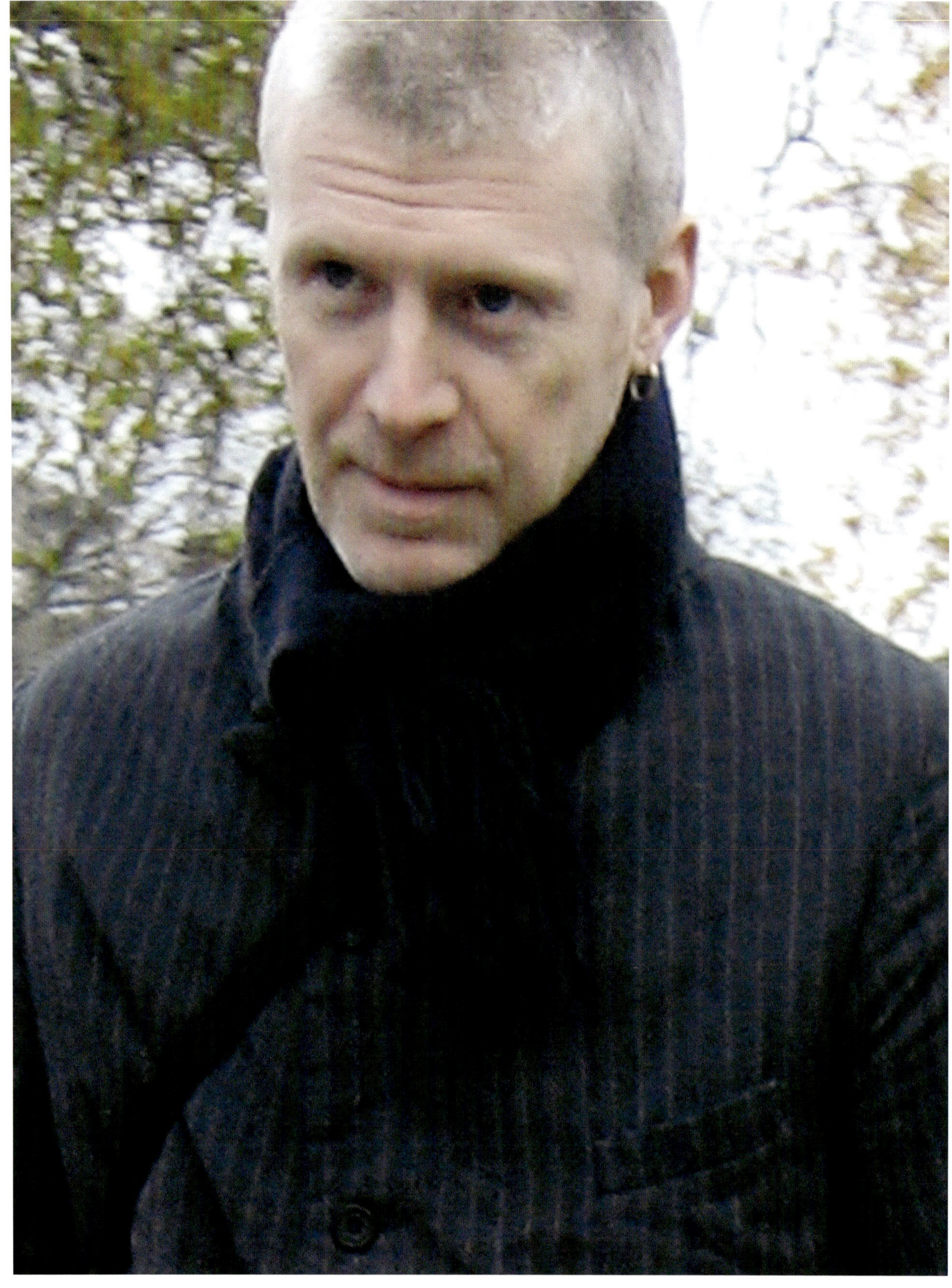

PAUL MORRISON PHOTOGRAPHY BY SUSIE PARRY

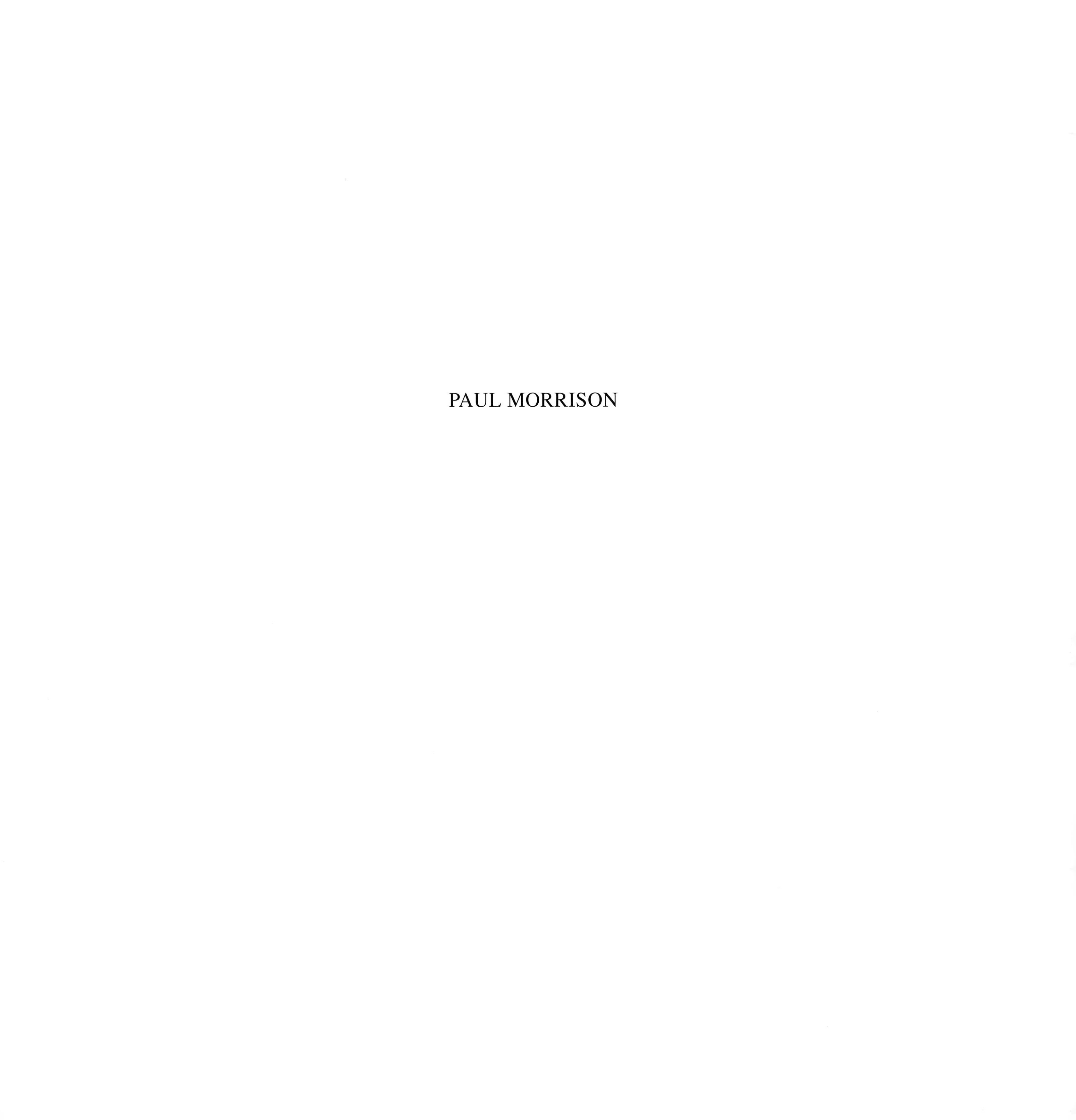

PAUL MORRISON

Paul Morrison

Opercullum, 2007

acrylic on linen

201 x 134 cm

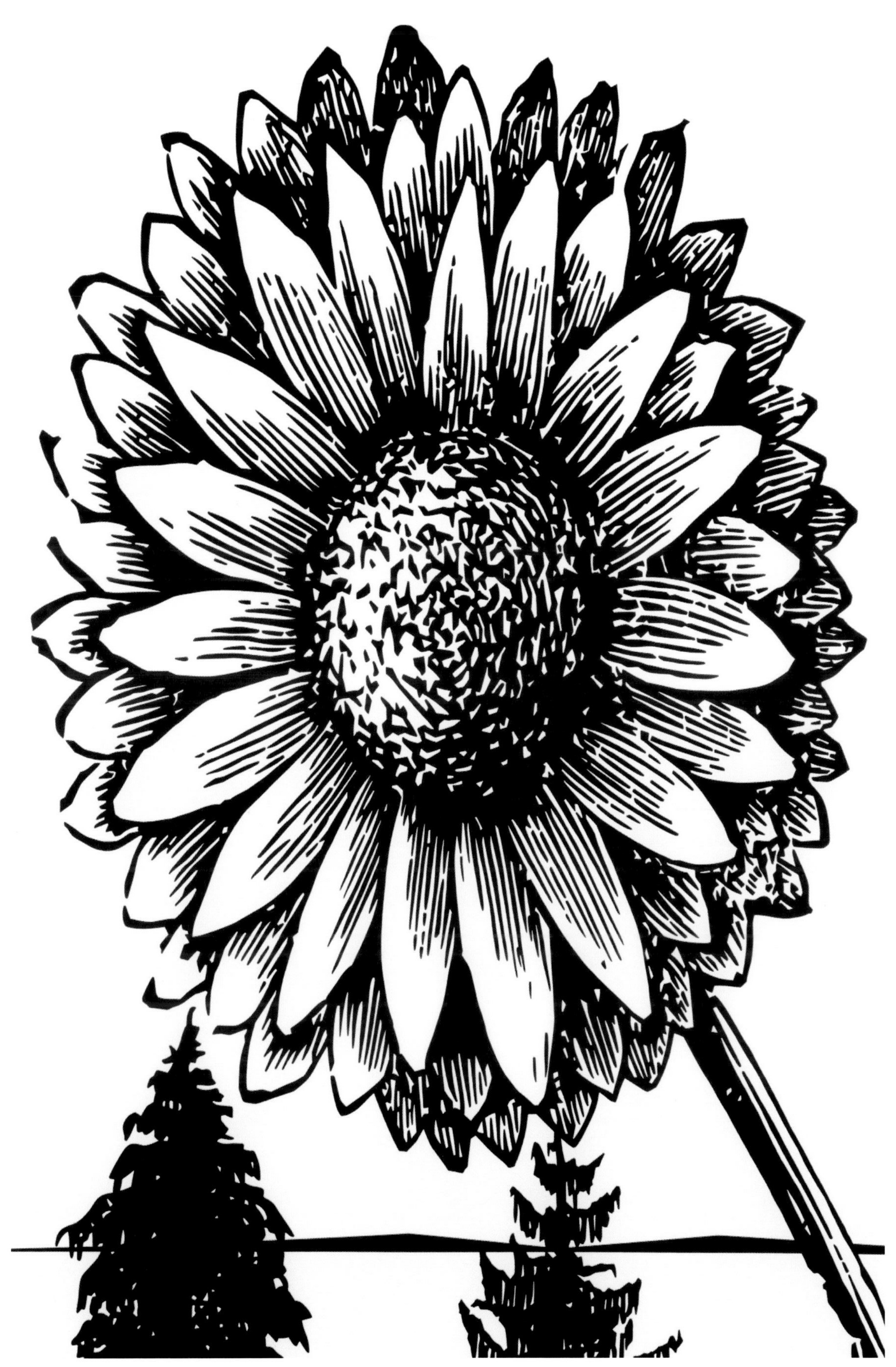

Paul Morrison

Trichome, 2007

acrylic on linen

144 x 180 cm

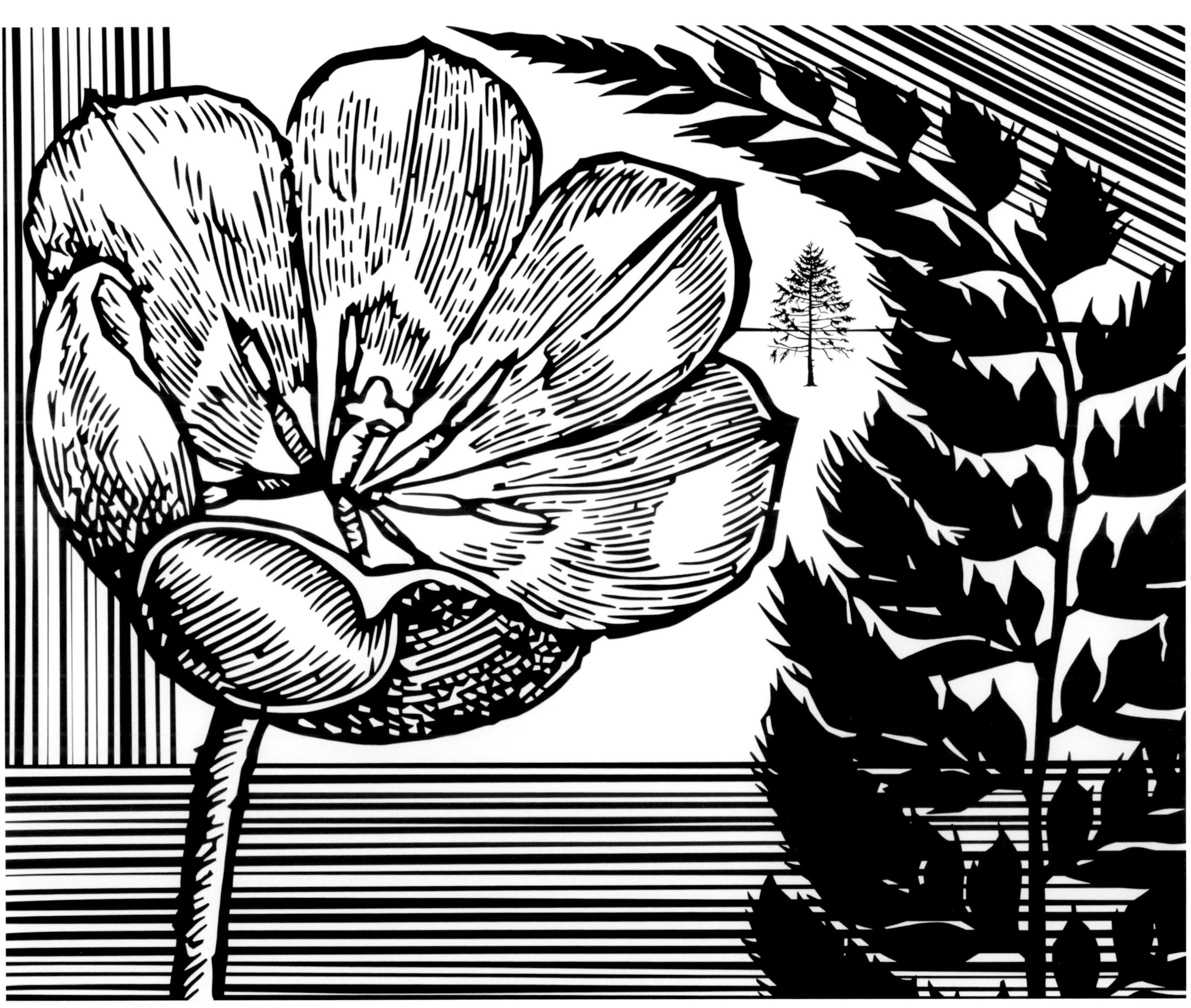

Paul Morrison

Propagule, 2007

acrylic on linen

128 x 160 cm

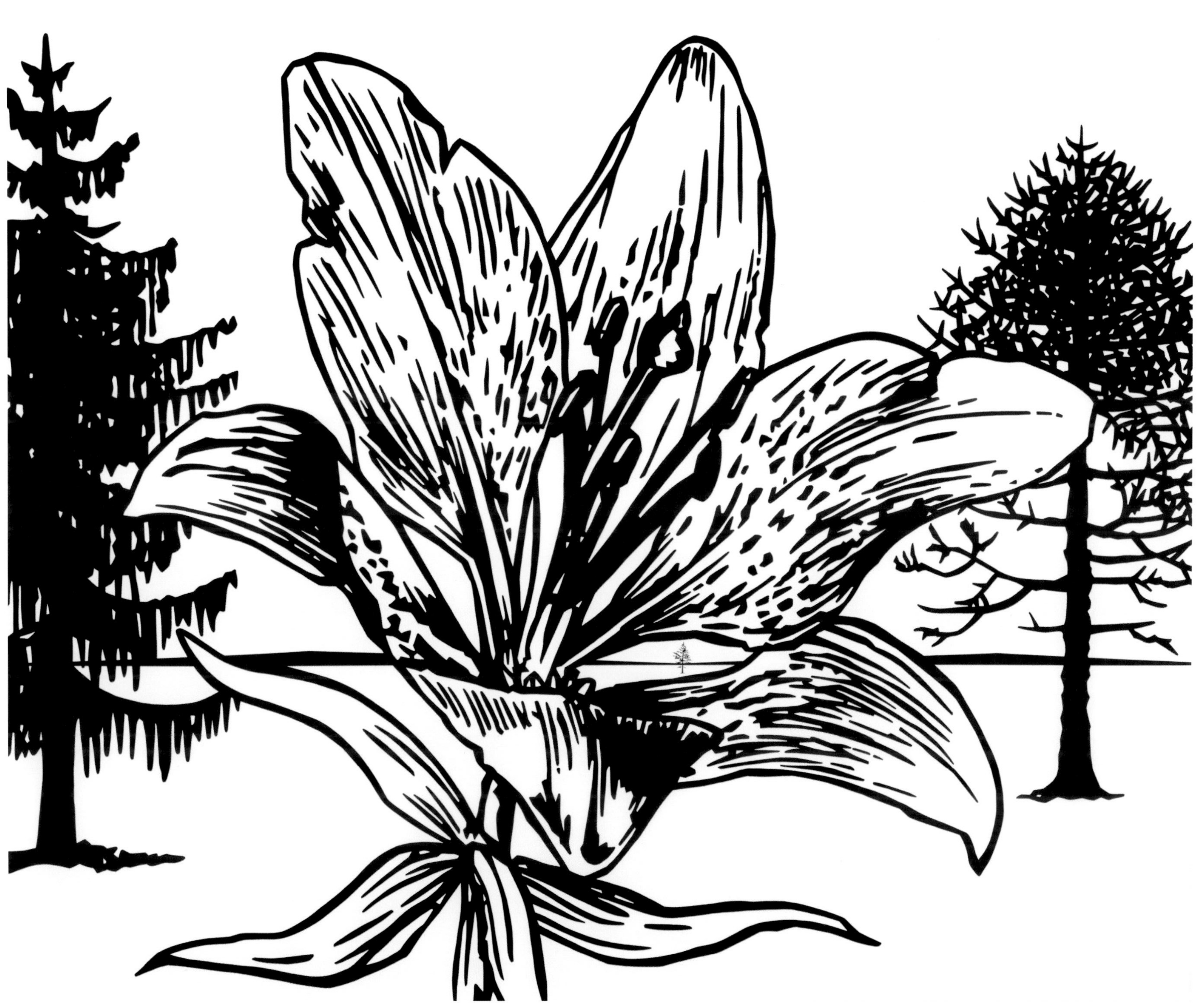

Paul Morrison

Siliqua, 2007

acrylic on linen

120 x 160 cm

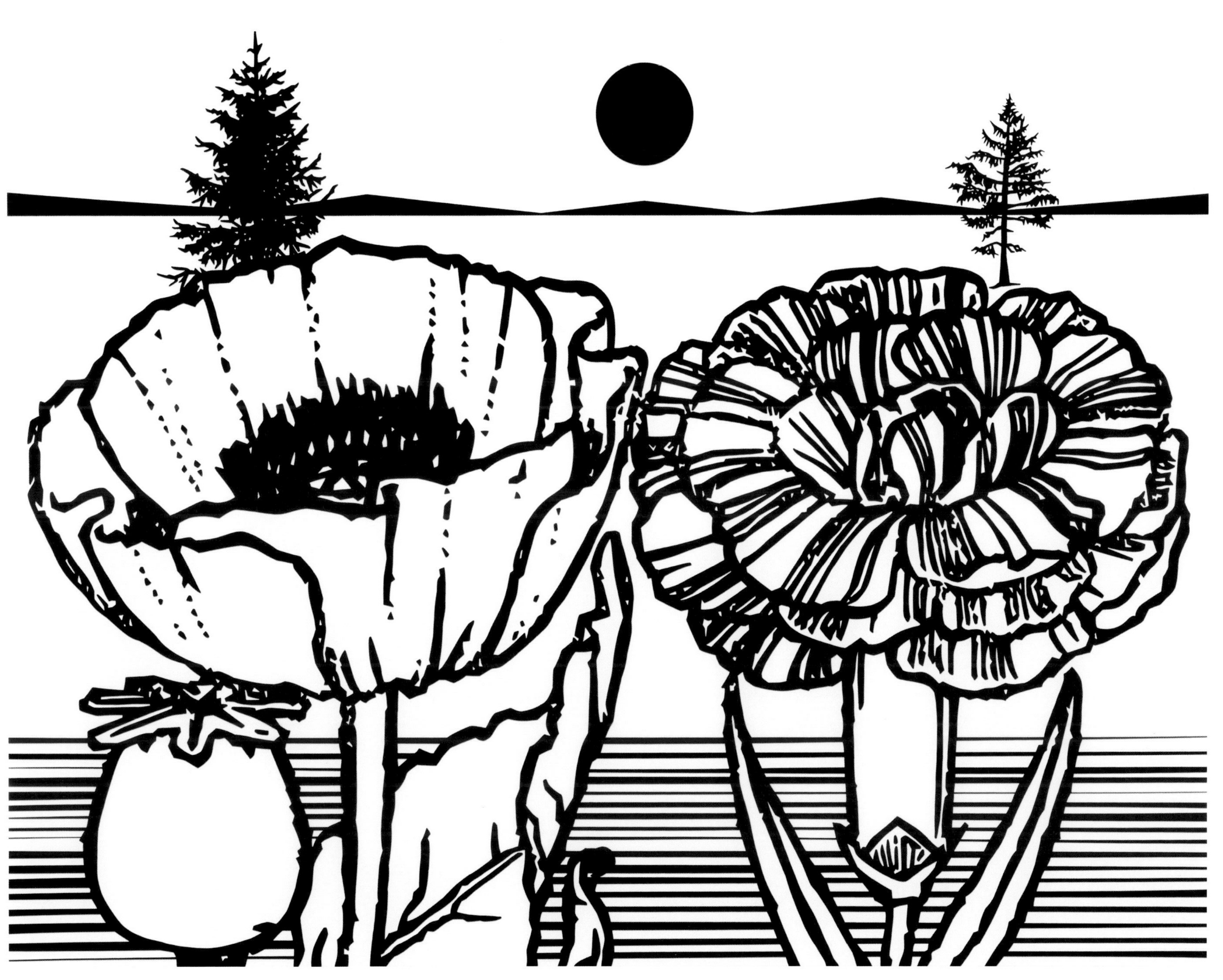

Paul Morrison

Geocarp, 2007

acrylic on linen

90 x 120 cm

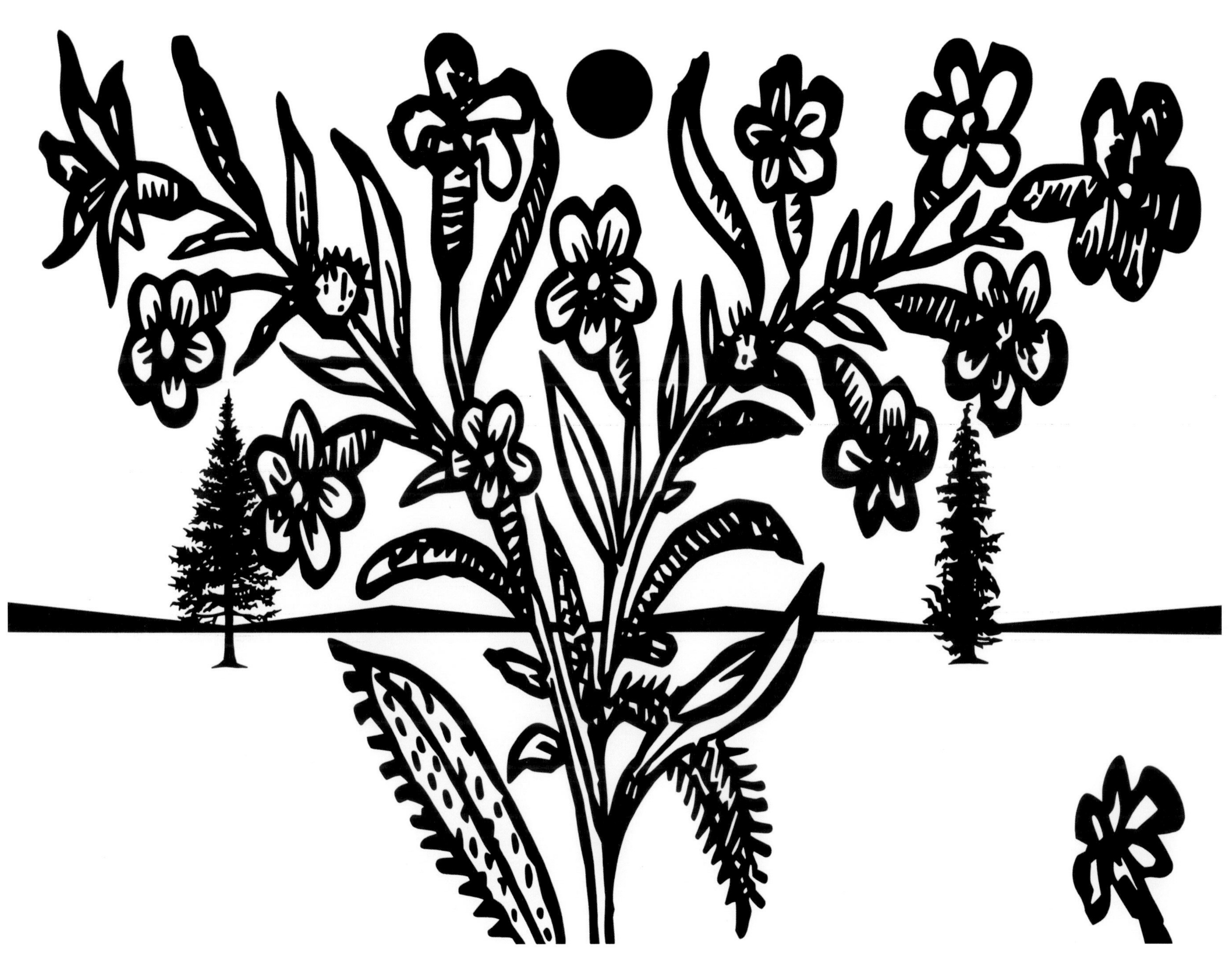

Paul Morrison

Fornix, 2007

acrylic on linen

120 x 80 cm

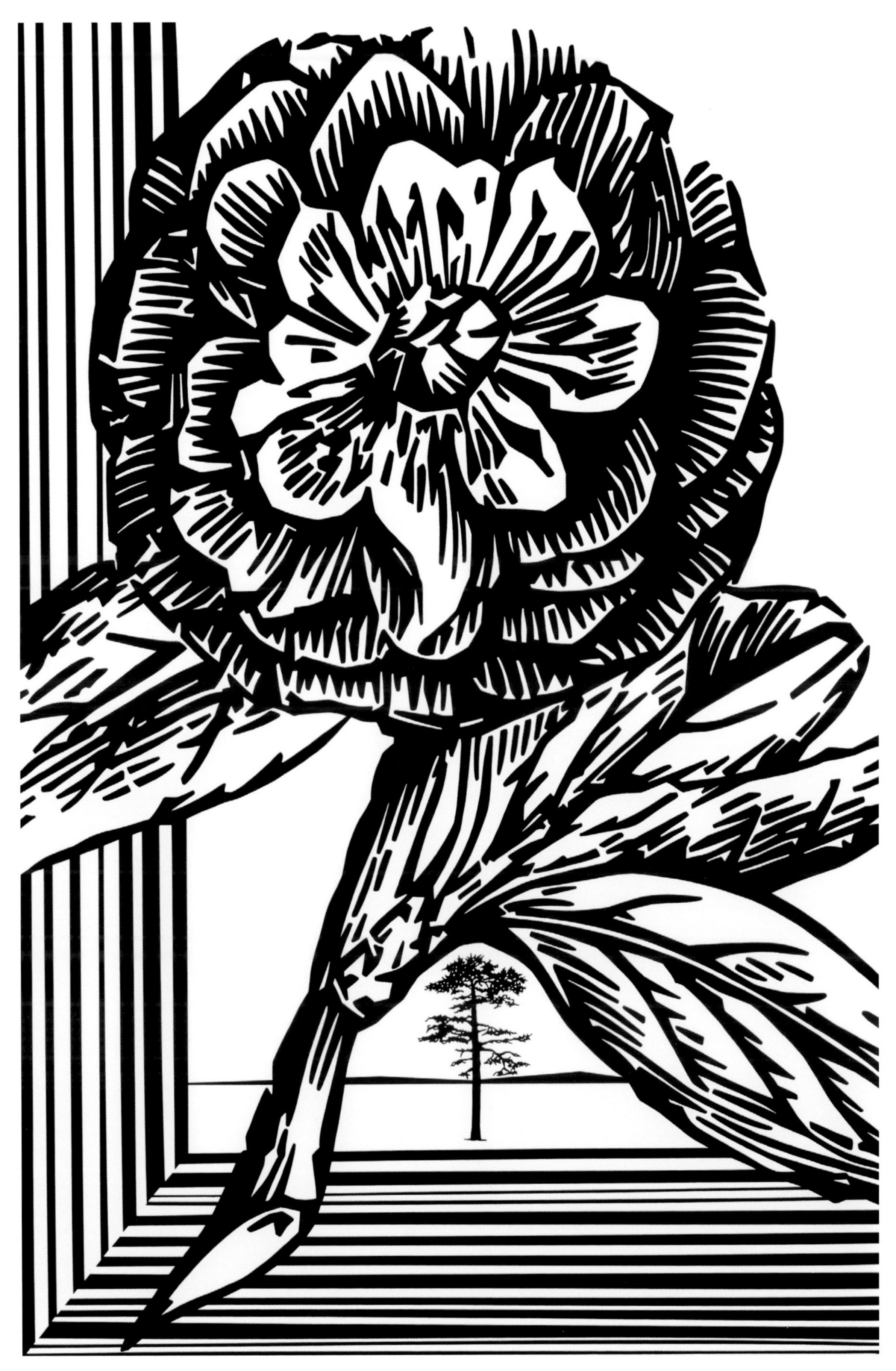

Paul Morrison

Phylum, 2007

industrial powder coated marine aluminium

and galvanised steel

55,5 x 34,5 x 0,6 cm

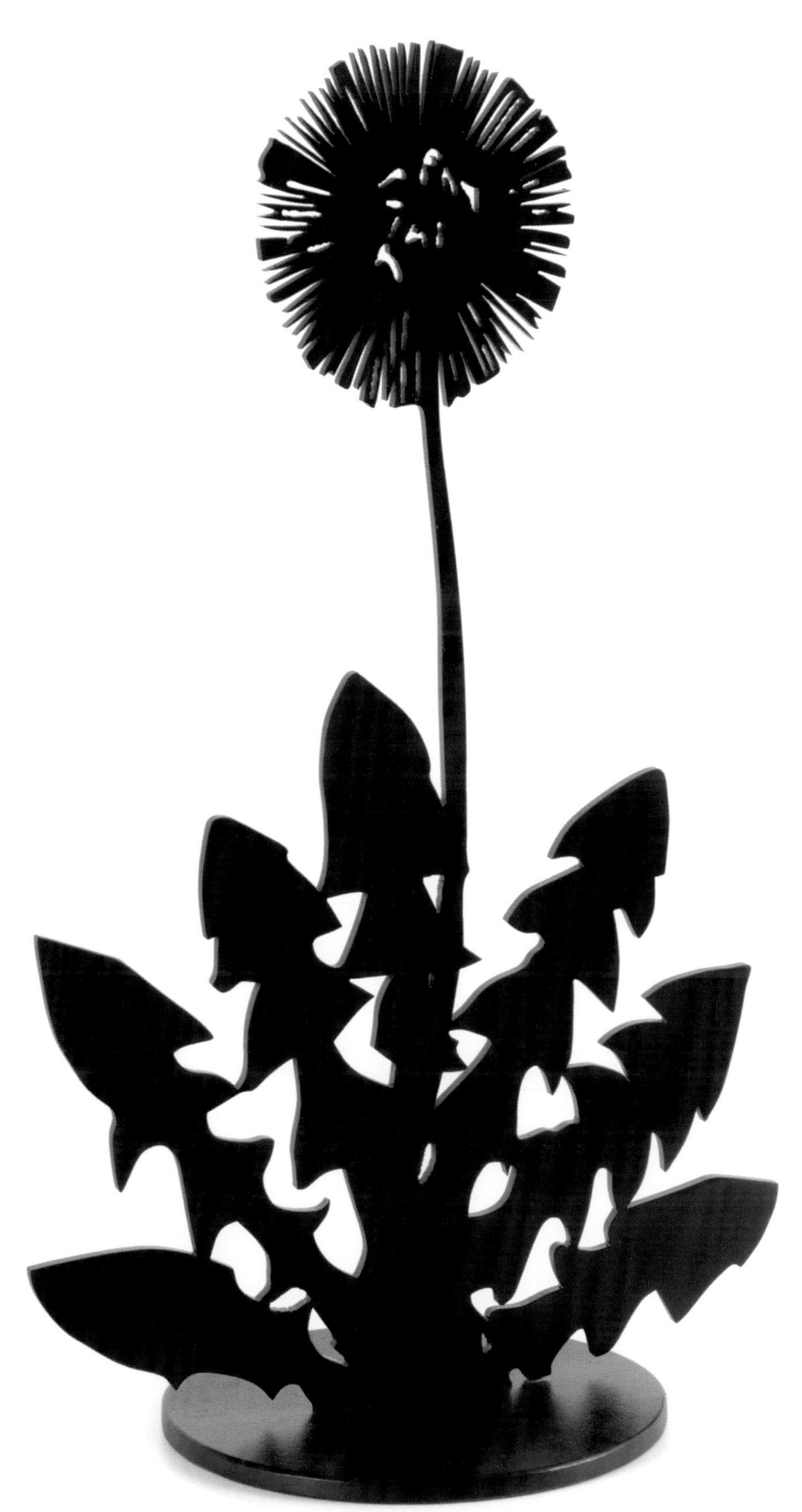

Paul Morrison

Topocline, 2007

industrial powder coated marine aluminium

and galvanised steel

57 x 50 x 0,6 cm

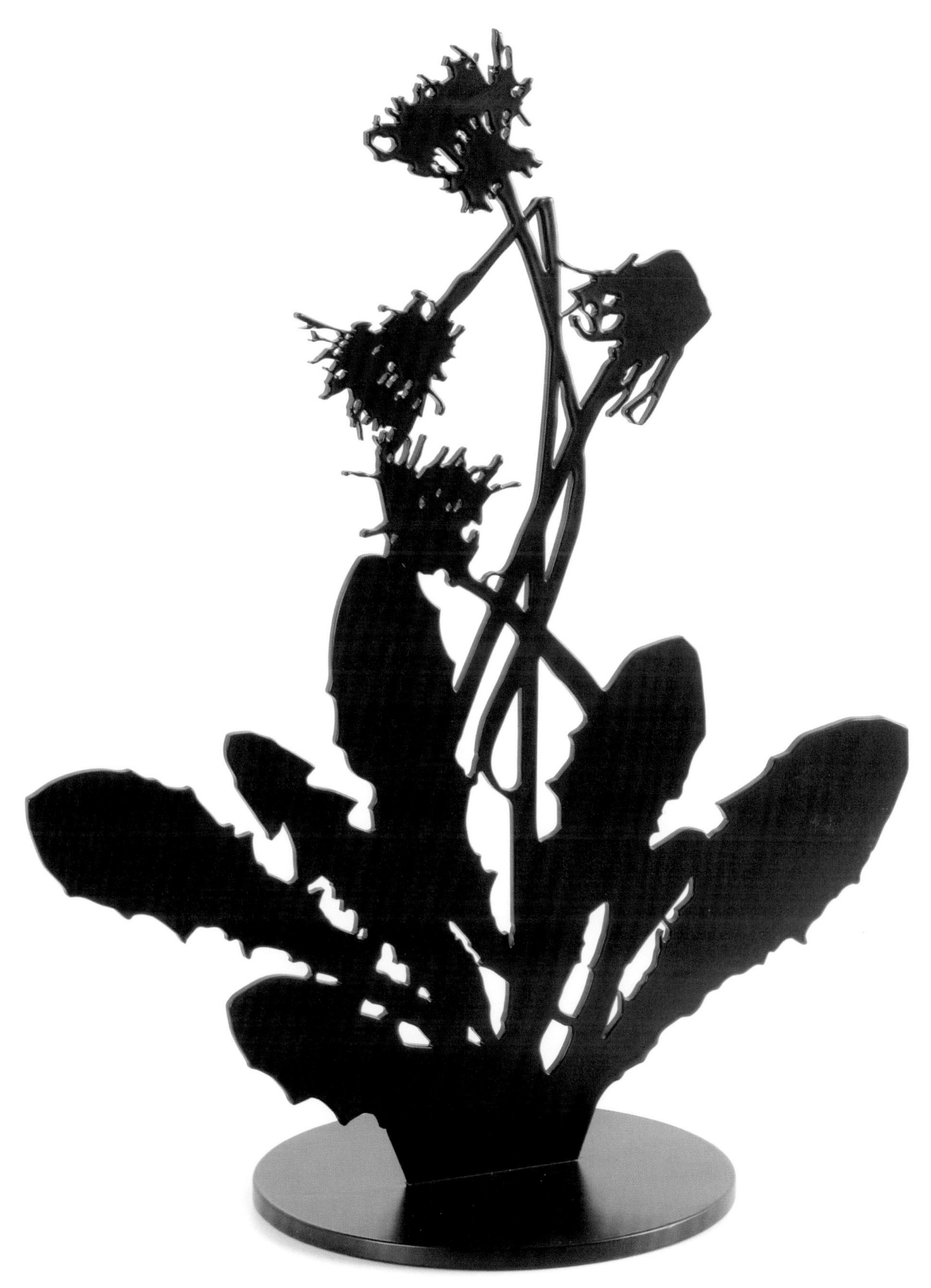

BIOGRAPHIES

DONALD BAECHLER

Born in Hartford, Connecticut 1956
Lives and works in New York City

EDUCATION

1978 – 79 Staatliche Hochschule fuer Bildende Kuenste, Staedelschule, Frankfurt am Aim, Germany
1977 – 78 Cooper Union, New York
1974 – 77 Marylnd Institute, College of Art, Baltimore

SELECTED SOLO EXHIBITIONS

2007 Galerie Thaddaeus Ropac. Paris, France
Museo Forte Strino. Vermiglio, Italy
Donald Baechler – New Works, Museum Moderner Kunst Kärnten MMKK, Klagenfurt, Austria
2006 Galleri Lars Bohman, Stockholm, Sweden
Donald Baechler , Cheim & Read, New York , USA
New Sculptures and Related Works, Galerie Thaddeus Ropac, Salzburg, Austria
Winter Sports, Ciasa de ra Regoles - Museo Rimoldi, Cortina d'Ampezzo, Italy
2005 *Paintings 1991- 2003*, Galerie Bernd Klüser, Munich, Germany
The Enemies of the Rose, Kunsthalle Merano, Italy
Sculpture, Cheim & Read, New York, USA
2004 *Sculptures*, Galerie Thaddaeus Ropac, Paris, France
Sculptures, Museum der Moderne, Rupertinum, Salzburg, Austria
Donald Baechler, Cardi, Milan, Italy
Baldwin Gallery, Aspen, USA
2003 *Donald Baechler*, Lars Bohman, Stockholm, Sweden
Donald Baechler, Cheim & Read, New York, USA
2002 *Principal & Auxillary Functions: Some Recent Pictures*, John Berggruen, San Francisco, USA
Galleria Leyendecker, Tenerife, Spain
2001 *Some of My Subjects*, Studio d'Arte Raffaelli, Trento, Italy
Oeuvres Récentes, Galerie Thaddaeus Ropac, Paris, France
Five Easy Pieces, Tony Shafrazi, New York, USA
2000 *Buildings and Other New Paintings*, Baldwin Gallery, Aspen, CO, USA
1999 *Globes and More*, Thaddaeus Ropac, Paris, France
Paintings from Kunsthalle, Basel, Tony Shafrazi, New York, USA
Crowd Paintings, Cheim & Read, New York, USA
1998 Galleria Civica di Arte Contemporanea, Trento, Italy

New Paintings, Kunsthalle Basel, Switzerland
Neue Bilder, Galerie Thaddaeus Ropac, Salzburg, Austria
1997 *Works on Paper*, Studio d'Arte Raffaelli, Trento, Italy
1995 *Works on Paper*, Paul Kasmin, New York, USA
Donald Baechler: Selected Early Paintings, Tony Shafrazi, New York, USA
Donald Baechler: Fish & Wildlife, Baldwin Gallery, Aspen CO; USA
Black Flowers, Bernd Klueser, Munich, Germany
1994 *Donald Baechler: 'des Fleurs'*, Thaddaeus Ropac, Paris, France
Donald Baechler: Drawings, Laura Carpenter Fine Art, Santa Fe NM, USA
1993 *Paintings, Works on Paper*, Sperone Westwater, New York, USA
Abstract Painting With Bird, Lars Bohman, Stockholm, Sweden
1992 *Works on Paper*, Gian Enzo Sperone, Rome, USA
1991 Anders Tornberg, Lund, Sweden
Max Hetzler, Cologne, Germany
Luhring Augustine Hetzler, Santa Monica CA, USA
1990 Gian Enzo Sperone, Rome, Italy
1989 Lucio Amelio, Naples, Italy
Flowers and Trees, Lars Bohman, Stockholm, Sweden
Tony Shafrazi, New York, USA
Works on Paper, Paul Kasmin, New York, USA
1988 *Donald Baechler: Paintings, Drawings & Prints*, Anders Tornberg, Lund, Sweden
Donald Baechler Paintings and Drawings, University Galleries, Illinois State University, USA
1987 Tony Shafrazi, New York, USA
1986 Larry Gagosian, Los Angeles, USA
New Paintings, Akira Ikeda, Nagoya, Japan
1985 Tony Shafrazi, New York, USA
Pat Hearn, New York, USA
1984 Tony Shafrazi, New York, USA
Neue Bilder, Ascan Crone, Hamburg, Germany
1983 Tony Shafrazi, New York, USA
1980 Studio Cannaviello, Milan, Italy
Artists Space, New York, USA

SELECTED GROUP EXHIBITIONS

2008 *Baechler – Morrison*, Gallery Alain Noirhomme, Brussels, Belgium
2007 *Four Friends*, Tony Shafrazi, New York, USA
Passion For Art: 35th Anniversary of the Sammlung Essl Collection, Sammlung Essl Collection, Klosterneuburg, Austria
2006 *Busy going crazy: collection Sylvio Perlstein*, La Maison Rouge, Paris, France
2005 *Figur Skulptur*, Sammlung Essl, Vienna, Austria

2004 *Visions of America*, Sammlung Essl, Vienna, Austria
Pop art & Minimalismus, Albertina, Vienna, Austria
2003 *Painting Lesson*, Galleria Cardi, Milan, Italy
Pictura Magistra Vitae, Fondazione Cassa di Risparmio in Bologna, Italy
2002 *Keine Kleinigkeit*, Kunsthalle Basel, Switzerland
Good News, Galleria Cardi &Co., Milan, Italy
2001 *Mythic Proportions: Painting in the 1980's*, MoCA Miami, USA
2000 *Painting*, Paul Kasmin Gallery, New York, USA
1999 *Selected Projects 1985-1990*, Baron/Boisanté, New York, USA
Peter Kogler, Ascan Crone, Hamburg, Germany
1998 *20 Years*, Galerie Bernd Klueser, Munich, Germany
Ensemble Moderne, Galerie Ropac, Salzburg & Paris, France
Dreams for the Next Century: A View of the Collection, Parrish Art Museum, Southampton NY, USA
Maps, Paul Kasmin Gallery, New York, USA
1997 *KünstlerInnen: 50 Positionen*, Kunsthaus Bregenz, Austria
1996 *Picasso: A Contemporary Dialogue*, Thaddaeus Ropac, Salzburg, Austria
Group Show, Tony Shafrazi, New York, USA
Works on Paper, Baldwin Gallery, Aspen CO, USA
1995 *Passions Privées*, Musée d'Art Moderne de la Ville de Paris, Paris, France
1995 'Yamantaka' Donation, Gagosian Gallery, New York, USA
Emblems and Contours, Sperone Westwater, New York, USA
1994 *Summer 1994*, Paul Kasmin, New York, USA
Summer Group Show, Sperone Westwater, New York, USA
1993 *New York On Paper*, Thaddaeus Ropac, Paris, France
1982-83 Ten Years After, Tony Shafrazi, New York, USA
The Spirit of Drawing, Sperone Westwater, New York, USA
Parallel Visions: Modern Artists and Outsider Art, Centro de Arte Reina Sofia, Madrid, Spain
Extravagant: The Economy of Elegance, Tony Shafrazi, New York, USA
Floor Show 'sculptures & objects', Anders Tornberg, Lund, Sweden
1992 *Ars Pro Domo 'Zeitgenössische Kunst aus Kölner Privatbesitz*, Museum Ludwig, Cologne, Germany
Der Gefrorene Leopard", Part II, Bernd Klueser, Munich, Germany
Group Sculpture Show, Sperone Westwater, New York, USA
Regard Multiple, Musée National d'Art Moderne, Centre Georges Pompidou, Paris, France
Sculpture, Paul Kasmin, New York, USA
1991 *Portraits on Paper*, Robert Miller, New York, USA
1990 *Vertigo*, Thaddaeus Ropac, Paris, France
The Last Decade: American Artists of the 80's, Tony Shafrazi, New York, USA
About Round/Round About, Anders Tornberg, Lund, Sweden
1989 *Einleuchten: Will, Vorstell und Simul in HH*, Deichtorhallen, Hamburg, Germany
1989 Biennial Exhibition, Whitney Museum of American Art, New York, USA
Repetition, Hirschl & Adler Modern, New York, USA

1988 *Art at the End of the Social*, Rooseum, Malmö, Sweden
Das Licht von der Anderen Seite I, Malerei, Monika Sprueth, Cologne, Germany

1987 XIX Bienal de Sao Paulo, Brazil
Terrae Motus, Grand Palais, Paris, France

1986 *What It Is*, Tony Shafrazi, New York, USA
Prospekt '86, Frankfurter Kunstverein/Schirn Kunsthalle, Frankfurt, Germany
Vom Zeichnen, Kunstverein Kassel, Germany & Museum Moderner Kunst, Vienna, Austria
Face It, Anders Tornberg, Lund, Sweden

1985 *Vom Zeichnen*, Frankfurter Kunstverein, Frankfurt, Germany
Pat Hearn, New York, USA

1984 *Works on Paper*, Peter Pakesch, Vienna, Austria

1983 *Accrochage: Gallery Artists*, Ascan Crone, Hamburg, Germany
Hundreds of Drawings, Artists Space, New York, USA
Champions, Tony Shafrazi, New York, USA

1982 Larry Gagosian, Los Angeles CA, USA
Donald Baechler/Ronnie Cutrone, Tony Shafrazi, New York, USA

1980 *Selections*, The Drawing Center, New York, USA
Arte para Los Ochenta, Galeria Durban, Caracas, Venezuela

PAUL MORRISON

Born in Liverpool, 1966
Lives and works in Sheffield and London

EDUCATION

1998 – 99 Goldsmiths College of Art, London, PhD Program
1996 – 98 Goldsmiths College of Art, London, MA Fine Art
1995 – 96 Goldsmiths College of Art, London, Postgraduate DIP Fine Art
1985 – 88 Sheffield City Polytechnic, Sheffield, BA (Hons) Fine Art

SELECTED SOLO EXHIBITIONS

2008 Las Vegas Art Museum, Las Vegas, USA
2007 Bloomberg Space, London, UK
PS, Amsterdam, The Netherlands
2006 The Contemporary Museum, Honolulu, Hawaii
2005 Sprüth Magers Projekte, Munich, Germany
Alison Jacques Gallery, London, UK
2004 Cheim & Read, New York, USA
2003 *Phenotype*, Michael Janssen, Cologne, Germany
Brake, Sprüth Magers Projekte, Munich, Germany
Saxifraga, Galleria d'Arte Moderna e Contemporanea, Bergamo, Italy
Haematoxylon, Irish Museum of Modern Art, Dublin, Ireland
PS, Amsterdam, The Netherlands
2002 *Mesophylle*, Magasin, Grenoble, France
Corymb, Kunstverein Ulm, Ulm, Germany
Cambium, aspreyjacques, London, UK
Bast, Art & Public, Geneva, Switzerland
Chloroplast, Southampton City Art Gallery, UK; Kunsthalle Nürnberg, Germany
2001 Karyn Lovegrove, Los Angeles, USA
Tomio Koyama + Taro Nasu, Tokyo, Japan
Wallworks: Ingrid Calame/Paul Morrison, Aspen Art Museum, Colorado, USA
Emmanuel Perrotin, Paris, France
Artspace, Auckland, New Zealand
2000 UCLA Hammer Museum of Art, Los Angeles, USA
PS, Amsterdam, The Netherlands
Carpenter Center for the Visual Arts, Harvard University, Cambridge, Massachusetts, USA

Philomene Magers Projekte, Munich, Germany
Forum Kunst, Rottweil, Germany
1999 Franco Noero, Turin, Italy
aspreyjacques, London, UK
Inverleith House, Royal Botanic Garden, Edinburgh, Scotland
Michael Janssen, Cologne, Germany
1998 Galerie Y-Burg, Amsterdam, The Netherlands
Site, Düsseldorf, Germany
1996 Habitat, King's Road, London, UK

SELECTED GROUP EXHIBITIONS

2008 *Baechler – Morrison*, Gallery Alain Noirhomme, Brussels, Belgium
2007 *neue editionen*, Sabine Knust - Galerie Maximilian Verlag, Munich, Germany
After Image, Two Rooms, New Zealand
Repicturing the Past/Picturing the Present, The Museum Of Modern Art, New York, USA
Door Cycle, Friedrich Petzel Gallery, New York, USA
Constallations II, Städel Museum, Frankfurt, Germany
It Starts From Here, De La Warr Pavilion, Bexhill on Sea, England
Fairy Tale, The New Art Gallery Walsall, touring to Chapter, Cardiff and Leeds City Art Gallery, UK
2006 *Eye on Europe: prints, books & multiples / 1960 to now*, The Museum of Modern Art, New York, USA
Boys and Flowers, Western Bridge, Seattle, USA
Broken Surface, Sabine Knust – Galerie Maximilian Verlag, Munich, Germany
Private View 1980/2000: Collection Pierre Huber, Musée cantonal des Beaux-Arts Lausanne, Switzerland
2005 *The Animators*, Angel Row Gallery, Nottingham (touring), UK
Painting The Edge, Gallery Hyundai, Seoul, South Korea
2004 *The Flower as Image*, Louisiana Museum of Modern Art, Humlebæk, Denmark
Satellite, ArtNow Lightbox, Tate Britain, London, UK
Flowers Observed, Flowers Transformed, the Andy Warhol Museum, Pittsburgh, PA, USA
3 Rooms 3 Artists, Alison Jacques Gallery, London, UK
Why Not Live for Art, Tokyo Opera City Art Gallery, Tokyo, Japan
The Boros Collection, ZKM Museum für Neue Kunst, Karlsruhe, Germany
Rose C'est La Vie, Tel Aviv Museum, Israel
Art of the Garden, Tate Britain, London, UK
Janssen feat. Janssen, Galerie Rodolphe Janssen, Brussels, Belgium
2003 *New Space! New Group Show!*, Galleria Franco Noero, Turin, Italy
Flower Power, Musée de Beaux-Arts, Lille, France
Lee 3 Tau Ceti Central Armory Show curated by Stéphane Magnin, Villa Arson Nice, France
Independence, South London Gallery, London, UK
Supernatural, Art on Demand Habitat, Hoxton Square, London, UK

Panorámica Programme, Museo Tamayo Arte Contemporáneo, Mexico
20th Anniversary Show, Monika Sprüth-Philomene Magers, Köln, Germany
Jun Hasegawa, Paul Morrison, Alessandro Raho, Taro Nasu Gallery, Tokyo, Japan
5 weeks, 5 Films, Max Hetzler Gallery, Berlin, Germany
John Moores 22 exhibition of contemporary painting, the Walker, Liverpool, UK
Interview with Painting, Fondazione Bevilacqua La Masa, Venice, Italy

2002 *The Drawing Center's 25th Anniversary Benefit Selections Exhibition Lottery*, The Drawing Center, New York, USA
Sphere, Soane Museum, London, UK
The Galleries Show, The Royal Academy of Arts, London, UK
The Jerwood Painting Prize 2002, Jerwood Space, London; Waterhall Gallery, Birmingham, UK
Melodrama, ARTIUM, Centro-Museo Vasco de Arte Contemporarneo, Vitoria; touring to the Palacio de los Condes de Gabia/Centro Jose *Guerroe*, Granada, Spain
Mapping the Process, Essor Gallery, London, UK
Animale, Vegetable, Minerale, Galleria Bonomo, Rome, Italy

2001 *Extreme Connoisseurship*, Fogg Art Museum, Cambridge, Massachusetts, USA
Effetto Natura curated by Mariuccia Casadio, Fondazione Nicola Trussardi, Milan, Italy
In fumo curated by Giacinto Di Pietrantonio, Galleria d'arte moderna e contemporanea, Bergamo, Italy
En pleine terre. Wandering between Landscape and Art, Spiral Jetty and Potsdamer Schrebergårten curated by Bernhard Mendes Bürgi, Museum für Gegenwartskunst, Basel, Germany
Tatoo Show, Modern Art, London, UK
Kyoto Portal, Invisible Museum, Kyoto, Japan
SchattenRisse: Silhoueten und Cutouts, Lenbachhaus, Munich, Germany
Freestyle, Museum Morbroich, Leverkusen, Germany
Bright Paradise, The 1st Auckland Triennial, Auckland Art Gallery Toi o Támaki with Artspace and The University of Auckland, Auckland, New Zealand
London Nomad, House of Zeinab, El Azhar, Cairo, Egypt

2000 Galeria Thomas Cohn, Sao Paolo, Brazil
ghosts, Delta Axis, Memphis, Egypt
00, Barbara Gladstone Gallery, New York, USA
I Believe in Dürer, Kunsthalle Nürnberg, Nürnberg, Germany
Twisted. Urban and Visionary Landscapes, Stedelijk Van Abbemuseum, Eindhoven, The Netherlands
Lemon Tree Hill, aspreyjacques, London, UK
Shout & Scream, Städitische Ausstellungshalle am Hawerkamp, Münster, Germany
www.blackandwhite.colour.3d.com, Gio' Marconi, Milan, Italy
Wooden Heart, Avco, London, UK
Wreck of Hope, The Nunnery, London, UK

1999 *Colour Me Blind!*, Württembergischer Kunstverein Stuttgart touring to StädtischeAusstellungshalle am Hawerkamp, Münster, Germany; *Dundee Contemporary Arts*, Dundee, Scotland, UK
John Moores 21 Painting Prize, Walker Art Gallery, Liverpool, UK
coming up for air, The Cooper Gallery, University of Dundee, Scotland, UK
Fresh Paint – Recent Acquisitions from the Frank Cohen Collection, Gallery of Modern Art, Glasgow, UK

Heart + Soul, 60 Long Lane, London; Sandroni / Rey Gallery, Los Angeles, USA
Down and Out in Paris and in London curated by Renaud Bézy, The Freak Brothers, Paris, France
Otros Retratos / Other Portraits, Galería Salvador Díaz, Madrid, Spain
Trouble Spot. Painting, Museum van Hedendaagse Kunst, Antwerp, Belgium
Protoplasm, Bob van Orsouw, Zürich, Germany
Cognitive Landscape, Dorothée De Pauw Gallery, Brussels, Belgium
infra-slim spaces, Invisible Museum loans to Birmingham Museum of Art, Alabama, USA
Selections Winter 99, The Drawing Center, New York, USA

1998 *Red Light District - Images of Desire*, Galerie Y-Burg, Amsterdam, The Netherlands
Whitechapel Open, Whitechapel Art Gallery, London, UK
Sunshine Breakfast, Michael Janssen, Cologne, Germany
Summer Show, The Trade Apartment, London, UK
Printemps, Deutsch Britische Freundschaft, London, UK
A Pub, Copperfield Road, London, UK
new contemporaries 98, Tea Factory, Liverpool, touring to: Camden Arts Centre, London; Hatton Gallery, Newcastle, UK
Landschaft, Trinkaus Galerie, Düsseldorf, Germany
Surfacing, Institute of Contemporary Arts, London, UK
dumbpop, Jerwood Gallery, London, touring to LMU Gallery, Leeds, UK

1997 *Fifty Quid*, Goldsmiths College, London, UK
Humdrum, The Trade Apartment, London, UK
World of Painting, Unit, London, UK
Underworld, The Australian Studio, London, UK

1996 *Whitechapel Open*, Whitechapel Art Gallery, London, UK
Gerard Hemsworth, Paul Morrison, Mike Stubbs, Suzy Willey, Villa Dei Cesari, London, UK

PUBLIC COLLECTIONS

British Council Collection, London, UK
Fitzwilliam Museum, Cambridge, UK
Fogg Art Museum, Harvard, USA
Government Art Collection, London, UK
MoMA, The Museum of Modern Art, New York, USA
Museum of Contemporary Art/Denver, Denver, USA
The Rhode Island School of Design Museum of Art, USA
Rubell Collection, Miami, USA
Southampton City Art Gallery, Hampshire, UK
Städel Museum, Frankfurt, D
Worcester City Art Gallery and Museum, Worcester, UK

BAECHLER – MORRISON

Catalogue and exhibition
Gallery Alain Noirhomme

Photographs of the artist by
Kevin Baker and Susie Parry

Photographs of the paintings
Philippe D. Photography and Donald Baechler Studio

Printed by
Graphic Production Cassochrome
Color Service Center

Books and catalogues available through
Editions Alain Noirhomme
Rue de la Régence 17 Regentschapsstraat
B-1000 Brussels
Tel 32 2 512 50 10   Fax 32 2 512 11 15
e-mail: lotus@skynet.be
www.alain-noirhomme.com

ISBN: 978-2-930487-04-5